ENTERING ADULTHOOD:

Understanding Depression and Suicide

ENTERING ADULTHOOD:

Understanding Depression and Suicide

A Curriculum for Grades 9-12

Nanette D. Burton, MA

Contemporary Health Series
Kathleen Middleton, MS, CHES, Series Editor

ETR Associates
Santa Cruz, California
1990

ETR Associates' Contemporary Health Series

Into Adolescence (for grades 5-8)

Choosing Abstinence
Enhancing Self-Esteem
Learning About AIDS
Learning About Reproduction and Birth
Living in a Family
A Time of Change (puberty)
Avoiding Drugs
Communicating Emotions
Becoming a Health-Wise Consumer
Making and Keeping Friends
Living Without Tobacco
Actions for Wellpower
Caring for Our Planet and Our Health
A Menu for Good Health
Fitness, Health and Hygiene
Stopping Violence

Entering Adulthood (for grades 9-12)

Connecting Health, Communication and Self-Esteem
Coping with Sexual Pressures
Living in Relationships
Preventing Sexually Related Disease
Understanding Reproduction, Birth and Contraception
Balancing Stress for Success
Understanding Depression and Suicide
Examining Drugs and Risks
Developing Responsibility and Self-Discipline
Planning Life Directions
Creating a Healthy Environment
Moving into Fitness
Looking at Body Image and Eating Disorders
Skills for Injury Prevention

Published by ETR Associates, P.O. Box 1830, Santa Cruz, CA 95061-1830.

Printed in the United States of America

10 9 8 7 6 5 4

Cover design: Julia Chiapella

Illustrations: Eric Berg

Title No. 391

Library of Congress Cataloging-in-Publication Data

Burton, Nanette.
    Entering adulthood: understanding depression and suicide /
Nanette Burton.
        p. cm. — (Contemporary health series)
    ISBN 1-56071-002-0
    1. Suicide—Study and teaching (Secondary) I. Burton, Nanette
    HV654.b 1990
    370.15'3—dc20   89-13305

This curriculum was made possible, in part, by a grant from the Walter S. Johnson Foundation. The opinions expressed in this curriculum are those of the author and do not necessarily reflect the opinions of the Walter S. Johnson Foundation.

CONTENTS

ACKNOWLEDGMENTS

The author wishes to acknowledge the contributions of Heartbeat, a suicide support group in Colorado Springs; La Rita Archibald; and S.P.A.R.E., a suicide prevention agency in Denver, in providing information for this module.

EDITOR'S PREFACE
Contemporary Health Series

Health educators and practitioners know that prevention of health problems is far more desirable than treatment. The earlier the knowledge and skill to make healthful decisions are instilled, the greater the chance a healthful lifestyle will be adopted. School is the logical place in our society to provide children, adolescents and young adults the learning opportunities essential to developing the knowledge and skills to choose a healthful life course.

The **Contemporary Health Series** has been designed to provide educators with the curricular tools necessary to challenge students to take personal responsibility for their health. The long-range goals for the **Contemporary Health Series** are as follows:

Cognitive. Students will recognize the function of the existing body of knowledge pertaining to health and family life education.
Affective. Students will experience personal growth in the development of a positive self-concept and the ability to interact with others.
Practice. Students will gain skill in acting on personal decisions about health-related life choices.

Within the **Contemporary Health Series** there are two curricular divisions: *Into Adolescence* for middle school teachers and *Entering Adulthood* for high school teachers. The *Into Adolescence* modules focus on several different health and family life topics. Modules addressing puberty, AIDS, the family, self-esteem, reproduction and birth, sexual abstinence, friendship, emotions, nutrition, fitness, consumer choices, the environment, violence and drug, alcohol and tobacco education have been developed by skilled author/educators.

Entering Adulthood modules address reproduction and contraception, responsibility, stress, depression and suicide, life planning, communication and self-esteem, AIDS and other STDs, relationships, sexual abstinence, fitness, body image, the environment, injury prevention and drug, alcohol and tobacco education.

All the authors are, or have been, classroom teachers with particular expertise in each of the topic areas. They bring a unique combination of theory, content and practice resulting in curricula which weave educational learning theory into lessons appropriate for the developmental age of the student. The module format was chosen to facilitate flexibility as the modules are compatible with each other but may stand alone. Finally, ease of use by the classroom teacher has driven the design. The lessons are comprehensive, key components are clearly identified and masters for all student and teacher materials are provided.

The **Contemporary Health Series** is intended to help teachers address critical health issues in their classrooms. The beneficiaries are their students, our children, and the next generation.

Kathleen Middleton, MS, CHES
Series Editor

INTRODUCTION

Suicide among young people has become an increasing mental health concern, as suicide rates among young people ages 15 to 24 have tripled over the past thirty years. For people in that age group, suicide was the third leading cause of death in 1986. During the same year, suicide was the second leading cause of death for 15- to 19-year olds and the sixth leading cause of death for 5- to 14-year-olds. In actual numbers in 1986, over 5,000 young people ages 15 to 24 committed suicide, while 250 young people ages 10 to 14 took their own lives (National Center for Health Statistics). In addition, for every actual suicide, it is estimated that in 1986 there were twenty suicide attempts by 15- to 19-year-olds (Alcohol, Drug Abuse and Mental Health Administration, 1989).

These alarming figures indicate serious problems among a growing number of our young people. Death by suicide is a many-faceted problem. It involves feelings of despair, hopelessness, futility and powerlessness and an ultimate choice against life, against hope, against a belief in self. Perhaps suicide is a problem of adjustment, alienation, adaptation and reaction to a rapidly changing world full of incongruities, complexities and inconsistencies. Perhaps suicide is an individual statement about the growing problems in our world. Whatever the reason, we have a problem with our youth taking their own lives.

Entering Adulthood: Understanding Depression and Suicide is aimed at increasing the awareness of depression and suicide. It is a curriculum for high school that focuses on suicide as a process. If one thinks of suicide as a process rather than an event, an interesting fact emerges: A process involves a series of steps, stages, events or occurrences. This means that there are points throughout the process at which intervention can take place. The concept of process allows for preventive actions. As a psychotherapist with fifteen years of clinical experience, I have come to see time and again how intervention can successfully act to change the direction of self-destruction.

The overall goal of this module is to increase awareness of the process of suicide and to promote intervention through education. Because we can no longer afford to turn our back on the uncomfortable issues that plague our country and our young people, communities, schools, parents and students all need to become aware of suicide and its causes and methods of prevention.

Education has before it an array of new challenges. We no longer teach only the basics of reading, writing and arithmetic. Educators are now being asked to address the most difficult problems that we face in today's world—the problems of AIDS, teenage pregnancy, sexual assault , abuse of alcohol and other drugs, potential nuclear disaster, environmental concerns, self-esteem and stress, as well as other important mental health issues such as depression and suicide.

Teachers are being asked to be specialists in areas that require years of preparation and multiple degrees. It is not possible for any one person, or even a group of people, to have the expertise available to address the varied concerns presented to educators. Programs need to offer information, structure and guidance to the teaching community for such challenges.

This module is intended to provide a framework and guidance to educators when addressing the problems of depression and suicide among their students. The scope of the module is prevention through education and informed intervention.

Program Implementation

The curriculum is designed not to be an answer in itself but rather to be part of a program that addresses awareness, education and intervention. The target audience for the learning activities is students in grades 9-12. These students need to be aware of the problem of suicide and the fact that most suicides are preventable. The information and skills they acquire during this program will positively influence their own mental health, as well as that of others whom they contact in their lives.

The most effective use of this module is within a four-part prevention plan of implementation in a school or district. The four components of a program implementation plan are community, school, parents and students. The importance of teacher training and the involvement of parents, school personnel and the community cannot be overemphasized. A **Program Implementation** plan is outlined in Appendix A.

Most of the *Understanding Depression and Suicide* module addresses the student. The seven lessons are designed to present important material that students can process and incorporate into their lives. Processing is necessary for personalization and incorporation in order to facilitate growth and change.

Ideally, lessons should be taught within a time frame of no more than three weeks, with two lessons per week. The program can be administered in a shorter time frame. However, there is too much material in the module to be absorbed in only one session.

Overview

Because the topic of suicide is so important and sensitive and evokes a wide range of emotions, it is important to establish a safe and caring classroom atmosphere at the beginning of the module. The first lesson uses a brainstorming session to establish groundrules to be posted throughout the learning activities. A worksheet polls students on the extent of their acquaintance with people who have threatened or attempted suicide. Students also begin a journal in which to record their feelings during the unit.

In Lesson 2 students discuss stress and its various properties. Through the illustration of a stress continuum, students see that stress is inevitable and can be a positive as well as a negative force.

Lesson 3 offers students a definition of depression along with an imagery activity that leads students to remember their experiences of feeling depressed. Using a worksheet that lists symptoms of depression, students work in small groups to develop and present a roleplay depicting depression. Lesson 4 deals with the causes of depression. Students discuss transparencies and worksheets that illustrate the factors contributing to feelings of loss and depression.

In Lesson 5 students use charts and worksheets to describe the breakdown of coping skills and the relationship of such a breakdown to stress, depression and suicide. Students also examine some common facts and myths about suicide.

Lesson 6 emphasizes the importance of recognizing verbal suicide warnings and offers several examples of such warnings. A class discussion of suicide risk is accompanied by a worksheet listing some of the risk factors of suicide. Students view the entire process that can lead to suicide risk and then create their own stories or artwork depicting an individual at risk.

The last lesson emphasizes the importance of personal resources and the tools of intervention. Students are encouraged to identify people in their own lives whom they can talk to about their feelings and to become acquainted with community resources. They are also urged to contact trusted adults for help if they suspect a suicide risk.

Objectives

Lesson 1	*Touched by Suicide*	■ Students will be able to explain the importance of studying about suicide.
		■ Students will be able to identify feelings associated with the concept of suicide.
Lesson 2	*Understanding Stress*	■ Students will be able to identify sources of stress.
		■ Students will be able to describe positive coping mechanisms for stress.
Lesson 3	*Understanding Depression*	■ Students will be able to describe signs and symptoms of depression.
Lesson 4	*Causes of Depression*	■ Students will be able to explain the importance of loss as a factor in depression.
		■ Students will be able to describe how life events and situations contribute to feelings of loss.
Lesson 5	*Understanding Suicide*	■ Students will be able to identify possible warning signs of suicide.
		■ Students will be able to describe how effective coping skills relate to stress, depression and suicide.
Lesson 6	*Determining Suicide Risk*	■ Students will be able to describe factors that determine suicide risk.
		■ Students will be able to explain why suicide is viewed as a process.
Lesson 7	*Intervention*	■ Students will be able to identify personal and community resources available in crises.
		■ Students will be able to describe appropriate actions to take when they suspect a suicide risk.

Instructional Strategies

This module incorporates a variety of instructional strategies to interest and involve students. Some strategies are traditional, while others reflect a more facilitative approach. This section describes (in alphabetical order) the instructional strategies used in this module.

Brainstorming   Overhead Transparencies
Class Discussion   Roleplays
Group Discussion   Worksheets
Mini-Lecture

Brainstorming

Brainstorming is used to open a discussion on an issue. Students are asked to give their ideas and opinions on a specific topic. They are also asked not to pass judgment on those ideas and opinions. The teacher's responsibility is to list on the blackboard or butcher paper everything that is said. Brainstorming should continue until all ideas have been exhausted or a predetermined time limit has been reached.

Class Discussion

A class discussion led by the teacher is one of the most valuable strategies used in education. It can begin a lesson, such as a brainstorming session, or it can end a lesson, being used to review and clarify the lesson's objectives. Nearly all the lessons in this curriculum include some form of class discussion.

Group Discussion

Group discussion is a process that uses small groups to disseminate information, analyze ideas or teach concepts to the rest of the class. This process also serves to increase student interaction. The size of the groups depends on the nature of the lesson and the make-up of the individual class. Generally, groups work best if they range from two to six members. The structure of the groups and the method of selecting groups will have an effect on the success of the lessons. There are a number of selection methods from which to choose: student selection, random selection or selection based on ability. Each method has its strengths and weaknesses. Once groups have been created, the process works best if all groups know the groundrules. It is suggested that while groups are working on their tasks, the teacher move from group to group to answer questions and deal with any problems that may arise.

Mini-Lecture

Mini-lecture is utilized to disseminate information directly from the teacher to the students. This method, combined with other instructional strategies, promotes high-level motivation and learning.

Overhead Transparencies

Overhead transparencies are used throughout the module as a visual strategy to present and review information and to provide graphic examples of work in which students will be involved.

Roleplays

Roleplays are highly motivating activities for students because they actively involve students in learning desired concepts or practicing certain behaviors. Students act out or act as if they are in a specific situation. Sometimes they are given a part to play, and other times they are given an idea and asked to improvise. Students should be allowed time to decide the action of the roleplay situation and how the roleplay will end. The time for roleplay should be limited to no more than five minutes.

Worksheets

In some lessons students are asked to complete worksheets. Sometimes the worksheets are completed individually to afford privacy. At other times completed worksheets are shared with a group or completed as part of a group process.

Teacher Responsibilities

As with other sensitive topics, the teaching of this module must be approached carefully and teacher training is highly recommended. Teachers must be aware of the maturity level of individual classes and be able to adjust lesson activities and content accordingly. The teacher should make an effort to involve the students' family members when appropriate.

The classroom atmosphere is critical to the success of teaching a module about depression and suicide. Teachers can establish classroom conditions and groundrules that are essential to a feeling of security, autonomy, belonging, purpose and personal competence. If possible, for discussions involving the whole class, seating should be arranged in a circle or horseshoe configuration so that all students can see their classmates. Such seating arrangements promote a more relaxed environment and encourage interaction.

Groundrules should be established to help provide a comfortable, positive and secure classroom environment. Some suggestions for groundrules follow.
- Listen carefully to others.
- Allow others to speak without interruption.
- Show respect for others.
- Do not make any judgments about any student's comments.
- Show respect for the seriousness of the subject matter.
- Do not bring up another person's personal history.
- Do not share any personal communications made in class outside the class.
- No put-downs will be allowed.
- Show sensitivity to others.
- Contributions made in class are to be voluntary.

Students should be assured from the beginning that they have the right to pass during any discussion or activity that involves personal opinions, feelings or experiences.

Note: Students are often very busy mentally and emotionally while listening to information on suicide. They are applying the information to their own lives or to the lives of people they care about.

Evaluative Methods

Each lesson provides the teacher with one or more methods for evaluating student performance on stated objectives. The methods are listed following the Procedure section of each lesson. Evaluative methods include analysis and comment on worksheets and other written materials, as well as observation of individual responses. It is impossible to objectively, quantitatively or qualitatively measure the development and maintenance of awareness and personal coping skills, and it is inappropriate to grade student work that is reflective of individual feelings, beliefs or behaviors. Therefore, the evaluation methods serve as tools to assess student participation and cognitive learning from each lesson.

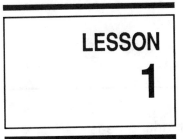

LESSON 1

TOUCHED BY SUICIDE

Objectives

Students will be able to explain the importance of studying about suicide.

Students will be able to identify feelings associated with the concept of suicide.

Overview

A topic as important and sensitive as suicide evokes a wide range of feelings, and it is important to establish a safe and caring classroom atmosphere at the beginning of the module.

In this first lesson students use a brainstorming session to establish groundrules for the class to follow. The groundrules will be posted throughout the module. Student worksheet responses indicate the extent to which students are acquainted with people who have threatened or attempted suicide. Students also begin a journal in which to record their feelings during the module.

Time

One 50-minute class period.

Teacher Materials and Preparation

HAVE:

✓ Butcher paper or poster board and marking pens.

COPY:

✓ **Touched by Suicide** worksheet for each student.

Key Points

➤ The topic of suicide is a sensitive one for both youth and adults.

➤ Groundrules help establish a level of comfort and safety with the subject.

➤ Journal entries are a personal and private way to identify feelings associated with the concept of suicide.

Procedure

■ Introduce the upcoming lessons on suicide. Explain to students that suicide is not an easy topic for most people. Students may feel a level of discomfort and should be reassured that such feelings are normal.

• Explain that when dealing with this subject in class, certain groundrules must be established to assist in the development of a level of comfort and safety for students. The atmosphere in the classroom should be safe, caring and respectful.

Ask students to brainstorm appropriate groundrules to be agreed upon by the class. Some possible groundrules are:

• Show respect for others. No one should make any judgments about any other student's comments.
• Show respect for the seriousness of the subject matter.
• It is not appropriate to bring up someone else's personal history.
• All personal communications made in class will remain private and are not to be shared outside the class.
• No put-downs will be allowed.
• Be sensitive to the feelings, opinions and ideas of others.
• Contributions made in class are to be voluntary.

Post the final, agreed-upon groundrules on poster board or butcher paper and keep them posted throughout the lessons.

■ Once the class has established groundrules, ask for volunteers to share any of the feelings that arise when dealing with this topic. List the feelings on the board and discuss as appropriate.

To assist in processing feelings about this topic, have students begin a journal. Ask them to write the word *suicide* in their journals and list the feelings that come to mind. You may want to write this unfinished sentence on the board to help students frame the list for their journals:
"The topic of suicide makes me feel..."

■ Establish the overall goals and rationale for these lessons. Explain that there is growing concern about the increase of suicide among young people. Suicide prevention requires understanding the problem and its causes, knowing the warning signs and knowing what to do if one suspects suicide. An important aspect of this program is to explore and practice effective life-coping skills. Skill in coping with the stresses, pressures, problems and crises that occur in life is an important key to suicide prevention.

■ Tell students that you are going to take a poll of how many students have been, in one way or another, touched by suicide. Distribute the **Touched by Suicide** worksheet and review the directions. Reassure students of their option *not to* identify feelings on the worksheet. Encourage students to identify their feelings about the questions in their personal journal if they don't want to reveal them on the worksheet.

Collect the worksheets and tally the yes responses to each question for the class. Present the final data to students. It is likely that most students will have some personal knowledge of suicide.

Explain to students that many people who have been touched by suicide experience a host of feelings, including guilt, sadness, anger, loss and despair. It is natural for people to feel they could have done more to prevent a suicide or a suicide attempt. Emphasize that we cannot control the actions of others. We can, however, learn what to do when we think a friend or family member may be suicidal.

Note: The tally of the yes responses on the **Touched by Suicide** worksheet may have to be discussed on a subsequent day to allow time to collect and tabulate data from the worksheets.

Evaluation

Have students write a paragraph on the importance of suicide prevention education and identify common feelings associated with the subject. Students should also note their expectations about any personal benefits from these lessons.

Touched by Suicide

Directions: Think about each of the following questions. Circle *yes* or *no* as appropriate. For any *yes* answers, list any feelings you have related to the question. (This section is optional.) All information will be held confidential. If you like, write any feelings you have about this activity in your journal.

1. Have you ever known someone who has said that he or she has *thought* about suicide as a solution to a problem?
   yes   no

   I felt...
   (optional)

2. Have you ever known anyone who has *attempted* suicide?
   yes   no

   I felt...
   (optional)

3. Have you ever known anyone who has *committed* suicide?
   yes   no

   I felt...
   (optional)

LESSON 2

UNDERSTANDING STRESS

Objectives

Students will be able to identify sources of stress.

Students will be able to describe positive coping mechanisms for stress.

Overview

In our modern society there are many pressures on teens. Understanding the role of stress in their lives and learning to cope with it in positive ways can help students avoid feelings of depression that, left untreated, can provoke thoughts of suicide.

In this lesson students discuss stress and its various properties. Through the illustration of a stress continuum, students see that stress is inevitable and can be a positive as well as a negative force. During a brainstorming session, students produce a list of sources of stress and then work in small groups to identify ways of coping with stress.

Time

One 50-minute class period.

Teacher Materials and Preparation

HAVE:
✓ Overhead projector.

OBTAIN:
✓ A classroom set of the pamphlet "Teen Stress" from Network Publications (optional).

MAKE:
✓ Transparency of **Coping Skills**.

COPY:
✓ **Positive Coping Skills** worksheet for each student.
✓ **Sources and Effects of Stress** worksheet for each student.

REVIEW:
✓ **Teacher Background Information**.

Key Points

➤ Stress is a part of life occurring in both positive and negative events.
➤ Reactions to stress differ from individual to individual.
➤ Some people feel stress more in their bodies, some in their thoughts and some in relation to their feelings.
➤ Distress is an emotionally upsetting influence.
➤ We can learn to effectively manage stress and to eliminate certain distress.
➤ Coping skills are life skills for handling, dealing with or managing stress and distress.

Procedure

■ Write the word STRESS on the board in large letters. Point out to students that stress is an important factor in suicide. People who think about, attempt or actually commit suicide have most likely had a difficult time dealing effectively with the stress in their lives.

Ask for volunteers to describe what stress feels like. Guide the discussion to help students conclude the following:
- Stress is different from individual to individual.
- Stress can be felt physically, mentally or emotionally.
- Stress is a normal aspect of life.
- The feeling of stress is sometimes described as a pressure, a weight, a tension, a heaviness, a tightness or even a stiffness.

■ On the board, to the right side of the word STRESS, write the word DISTRESS, as follows:

STRESS $\longleftrightarrow$ DISTRESS

Explain that as stress builds up and individuals begin to have difficulties, stress can become very negative. This is sometimes termed *distress*. Distress can be defined as an upsetting influence. Point out that distress is also a normal part of life. The important thing to learn is how to cope with distress (or stress buildup) in order to find a sense of balance and personal self-worth. This is sometimes called *centering*, finding a place where one feels whole, complete and comfortable. Life is a process of balancing toward wholeness and comfort with oneself.

■ On the board, to the left of the word STRESS, write the word EUSTRESS, as follows:

EUSTRESS $\longleftrightarrow$ STRESS $\longleftrightarrow$ DISTRESS

Point out that even the good things in life are stress producing. Feeling excitement about an important date, playing in the "big game" next week and qualifying for an honors class are all examples of situations that can be stressful. "Good stress" is sometimes called *eustress*. It stimulates all the same physical, mental and emotional reactions as stress or distress.

■ Have students brainstorm possible sources of stress in one's life. List them on the board. They may include the following:
- school expectations
- home and family experiences
- work responsibilities
- sports involvement
- emotional health
- sibling relationships

- relationships with other relatives
- relationships with boyfriends and girlfriends
- home chores and responsibilities
- physical health
- future goals
- traumatic life experiences
- wishes, dreams and expectations about life
- disillusionment in others or oneself

The list can go on and on. Almost anything in life has the potential to produce stress.

Teacher Background Information on the sources and effects of stress can be used to augment this discussion.

Option: The pamphlet "Teen Stress" from Network Publications can be used as a resource for this discussion. It is fully illustrated and appealing to teens.

■ Write COPING SKILLS on the board. Explain that these are things we do to manage stress in our lives. We all have various ways we cope with things that are stressful. Use the **Coping Skills** transparency as a basis for discussion of the difference between positive and negative coping behaviors.

Divide students into groups of four or five and distribute the **Positive Coping Skills** worksheet. Ask students to identify some situations that might cause stress and discuss positive ways to cope with them. Then have volunteers from each group report on the group's discussion.

Evaluation

Have students list on a blank sheet of paper at least three sources of stress in their lives. Then for each source, have them identify a positive coping skill that they will be willing to practice throughout this module. Have them also name someone they know who can serve as a resource or a source of support to them. Review student papers, assessing their ability to identify sources of stress and positive coping skills for the stress.

Ask students to use their journals to keep track of their use of the coping skills they have identified.

Teacher Background Information
Sources and Effects of Stress

Where Does Stress Come From?

Stress can originate anywhere. Stress is different for every individual. What one person feels to be stressful might not affect another.

The following are the most common areas that produce stress:

◆ *Employment*
Having a job, not having one, losing one, at-work pressures, salary expectations, job satisfaction, employment expectations

◆ *School*
Teacher expectations, tests and grades, parent expectations of school performance, personal expectations, peer relationships, reciting in class, homework

◆ *Family*
Any conflict or unhappiness in the family: parent quarreling, family violence, child abuse, relationships with brothers and sisters, relationships with parents or other relatives, family communication styles, discipline styles, parent abuse of alcohol or other drugs

◆ *Relationships with Others*
Friendships, lack of friendships, what others think and feel, satisfaction with relationships

◆ *Physical Health*
Any concerns about real or imagined health problems (physical health problems can produce physical and psychological, or mental, stress)

◆ *Physical Appearance*
Any concerns about how you look, including real or imaginary problems or flaws

◆ *Emotional Health*
How you feel about yourself, difference between how you see yourself and the way others see you, changes in how you feel about yourself from time to time

◆ *Outside Events*
Many other sources of stress exist, from flat tires to oversleeping.

What Can Stress Lead To?

◆ Stress has been linked with many physical illnesses and diseases.

◆ Stress can be viewed as an important factor in causing an illness, a result of an illness or a factor that stands in the way of recovery from an illness.

◆ The following physical illnesses are strongly linked with stress:

Allergic disorders
Anorexia nervosa
Asthma
Bulimia
Cancer
Certain neurological disorders, including
   epilepsy and brain tumors
Colitis
Dermatologic disorders

Diabetes
Fibrocystic breast disease
High blood pressure
Immunological disorders, including colds,
   flu, susceptibility to viral infections
Nutritional and metabolic disorders
Ulcers
Vaginitis
Yeast infections

◆ Stress is also linked to mental illnesses and disorders. An individual's responses to stress can combine with that person's genetic, environmental and psychological predispositions to create a climate for illness to occur or to continue.

◆ If stresses are intense enough and occur over a long enough period of time, people are at risk for stress to manifest itself in a physical or psychological form.

What Can We Do About Stress?

Recognize the stress in your life. What are the pressures you live with?

◆ We cannot eliminate stress from our lives, but we can learn to manage the stress we do experience and to eliminate some distress. We can accomplish this in part through active decision making and good mental health practices.

◆ Keep in mind that we cannot control things outside ourselves (job, school, family, health, weather), but we can control the ways we choose to react to those things.

COPING SKILLS

The following are some **positive** or **healthy** ideas for coping:

◆ talking to someone who cares

◆ exercise (jogging, walking, weightlifting, bicycling, etc.)

◆ sports

◆ reading a good book

◆ listening to music

◆ going shopping or buying something for yourself

◆ doing something nice for someone else

◆ talking to or spending time with pets

◆ watching a good movie

◆ spending time with a friend or friends

◆ going to your special place to think

◆ developing a sense of humor

◆ finding the humorous side to predicaments

The following are **negative** or **unhealthy** ways people cope:

◆ alcohol or other drug abuse

◆ driving fast

◆ promiscuity (being sexual without regard to whom you are with)

◆ self-mutilation (cutting, scratching oneself, scratching until bleeding occurs, pulling out hair, bruising yourself, self-tattoos, etc.)

◆ isolation of self from others

◆ excessive risk taking

Positive Coping Skills

Ways to reduce stress

☞ Talk to someone who cares.

☞ Exercise (jog, walk, lift weights, bicycle, etc.).

☞ Play sports.

☞ Read a good book.

☞ Listen to music.

☞ Go shopping or buy something for yourself.

☞ Do something nice for someone else.

☞ Talk to or spend time with pets.

☞ Watch a good movie.

☞ Spend time with a friend or friends.

☞ Go to your special place to think.

☞ Develop a sense of humor.

☞ Look for the humorous side to predicaments—there usually is one.

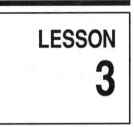

LESSON 3

UNDERSTANDING DEPRESSION

Objective

Students will be able to describe signs and symptoms of depression.

Time

One 50-minute class period.

Overview

The signs and symptoms of depression occur on a continuum—from mild feelings of sadness or grief, which everyone experiences at some time, to clinical depression, a serious behavioral or emotional pattern in which several symptoms of depression are exhibited over a prolonged period.

In this lesson students are offered a definition of depression; an imagery activity then leads students to remember their own experiences of feeling depressed. Using a worksheet that lists symptoms of depression, students work in small groups to develop and present a roleplay depicting someone who is depressed.

Teacher Materials and Preparation

COPY:

✓ **Symptoms of Depression** worksheet for each student.

✓ **Symptoms of Clinical Depression** worksheet for each student.

Key Points

➤ Depression is a condition—a combination of feelings, signs and symptoms. Stress is usually an important factor in the condition.

➤ Depression is trackable and is part of a process. (It doesn't just happen.)

➤ Symptoms of depression vary widely from individual to individual.

➤ A person suffering from clinical depression usually evidences at least four symptoms persisting nearly every day for at least two weeks.

➤ Some depression is normal. Usually we call this sadness or grieving.

➤ Grieving is a process of coming to terms with loss or losses. It is different from depression, as is sadness, although sadness may be a key component in the grieving process.

Procedure

■ Introduce the lesson by explaining that one result of stress buildup or continued distress is a condition called depression. Acknowledge that this subject is often not easy to think about or discuss. Tell students that it is normal to feel uncomfortable and even to feel some sadness as they consider what depression means to them or to others they care about.

Define depression for students, indicating that it is a combination of feelings, signs and symptoms. Depression is a word that describes certain feelings. It can be defined as a condition characterized by an inability to concentrate, insomnia, and feelings of dejection, guilt, sadness and worthlessness.

As appropriate, clarify this definition by discussing the meanings of *insomnia, guilt, dejection, sadness* and *worthlessness.*

■ Explain that it is normal to experience short-term bouts of depression. Such experiences are often called sadness or grief. Sadness and grief are usually associated with feelings of loss. Sadness and grief that result from the experience of loss are part of what it means to be alive. These feelings are normal. When feelings of sadness and grief continue and intensify, they can lead to depression. Tell students that they probably already know a lot about depression and that they probably have felt depressed at one time or another in their lives.

Conduct a brief imagery activity with students. Ask them to try to remember what depression feels like. Ask them to sit and relax, close their eyes and concentrate on their breathing. When you sense that most students are in a fairly relaxed state, ask them to think about a situation where they felt depressed. Have them remember the circumstances that were associated with being depressed and how their body felt. Give students about a minute to recall the feeling and the situation. In a very calm voice tell students to stay quiet, open their eyes and take several long, deep breaths.

Ask if any volunteers want to share any aspect of this experience. Conclude the activity by telling students that just as we have used a form of relaxation and visualization to recall depressed feelings, we can use the same technique to recall happy feelings.

Note: It is important to leave students with positive images. If time permits conduct the same activity with students visualizing a happy experience. Explain that this technique can be used effectively to cope with stress.

■ Distribute the **Symptoms of Depression** and **Symptoms of Clinical Depression** worksheets. Review the symptoms with the class and emphasize the definition of clinical depression. As necessary, clarify the meaning of various terms on the worksheet.

■ Divide students into groups of four or five. Ask each group to prepare a roleplay that dramatizes a situation in which someone appears depressed.

Give groups approximately ten minutes to prepare their roleplays, and have each group present its roleplay to the class. After each presentation have the class identify the symptoms presented, comment on how realistic the situation is and discuss possible coping skills that could be used in the situation.

Note: If time does not permit all groups to present their roleplays in one class period, be sure to have the remaining presentations made at another time.

Evaluation

Have students write a paragraph about an adolescent who exhibits signs of depression. Students should explain how the situation described illustrates clinical depression, as opposed to sadness or grief.

Symptoms of Depression

Depression describes a person's mood, how one feels. When we talk about depression, we are talking about a feeling.

Symptoms of depression include the following:

✖ negative or antisocial behavior

✖ wanting to leave home

✖ feelings of not being understood or approved of

✖ restlessness, grouchiness, sulkiness, aggression

✖ unwillingness to cooperate in family projects

✖ withdrawal from social activities

✖ hiding out in one's room

✖ school difficulties, including poor grades, not getting along with teachers and peers

✖ inattention to personal appearance

✖ extreme or sudden mood changes

✖ sensitivity to rejection, especially in love relationships

✖ abuse of alcohol or other drugs

✖ sexual promiscuity

✖ weight loss or weight gain

✖ sleeplessness or sleeping more than normal

✖ physical agitation or restlessness

✖ dragging around, slow physical movements and responses

Early symptoms of depression also include general feelings of anxiety, panic or fear.

Symptoms of Clinical Depression

To classify a person as clinically depressed, at least four of the following symptoms need to be present nearly every day for a period of at least two weeks.

✖ poor appetite, significant weight loss when not dieting

✖ increased appetite, significant weight gain

✖ insomnia or hypersomnia (inability to fall asleep or need for excessive amounts of sleep)

✖ physical agitation—a jumpy, nervous, twitching, restless body

✖ slowed physical body movements, no "spunk," dragging around

✖ loss of interest or pleasure in usual activities (not able to have fun)

✖ apathy (an "I-don't-care" attitude)

✖ loss of energy, fatigue

✖ feelings of worthlessness or excessive feelings of guilt and self-blame

✖ inability to think or concentrate, slowed thinking and/or inability to make decisions

✖ frequent thoughts of death or suicide, death wish or suicide attempt

CAUSES OF DEPRESSION

LESSON 4

Objectives

Students will be able to explain the importance of loss as a factor in depression.

Students will be able to describe how life events and situations contribute to feelings of loss.

Time

One to two 50-minute class periods.

Overview

There are many factors in depression, but feelings of loss play a major role, often evoking feelings of powerlessness or helplessness. When not dealt with, these feelings can lead to despair or to a type of trapped, unexpressed, immobilized anger, either of which can result in depression.

In this lesson transparencies and worksheets illustrate the factors that contribute to depression. Other activities encourage students to identify coping skills they can use in life situations that evoke feelings of loss.

Teacher Materials and Preparation

HAVE:
✓ Overhead projector.

MAKE:
✓ Transparency of **Contributing Factors**.
✓ Transparency of **Turning Loss Around**.

COPY:
✓ **Life Factors and Loss Feelings** worksheet for each student.
✓ **Help for Depression** worksheet for each student.

REVIEW:
✓ **Teacher Background Information**.

Key Points

➤ Usually there is not just one cause of depression.
➤ Depression can be physical (organic), having its origin in the body's biochemistry; or it can be functional, having its origin in the individual's environment.
➤ Environmental factors include psychological stressors (e.g., divorce, major illness, alcoholism in family) and traumatic events (e.g., death of a loved one, incest, rape).
➤ Most often, the first occurrence of a major depression takes place before age 30, and depression may recur throughout one's life.
➤ Environmental factors, including psychological stressors and traumatic events, have one important element in common—the element of loss.
➤ Feelings of powerlessness or helplessness become more likely to occur as losses multiply.
➤ Feelings of powerlessness may lead to the trapped feeling of despair, which may result in depression.
➤ Often depression results from a type of trapped, unexpressed, immobilized anger. Without a way to release this anger, individuals may turn the anger that belongs outside on themselves.
➤ Even when available resources exist, most young people do not consider contacting a professional for help with depression.

Procedure

■ Remind students that there is no one cause of depression; however, causes of depression fall into two main categories. *Physical* (or organic) causes are genetic, often rooted in the body's biochemistry. *Functional* causes are related to one's environment. Things in one's environment may act to increase stress and create a situation in which depression develops.

Use the **Contributing Factors** transparency to further discuss the causes of depression. Describe and clarify environmental factors, including family stressors and traumatic events. Use **Teacher Background Information** for reference.

■ Display the **Turning Loss Around** transparency and explain that feelings of loss do not have to result in depression or suicide risk. With practice we can learn to accept the losses that life deals and find strength and power in getting through painful times. This is certainly easier to say than to put into practice. But the establishment of effective coping skills for stress will help us accept loss and feel powerful when we survive these feelings.

Distribute the **Life Factors and Loss Feelings** worksheet. Ask students to describe the way certain life events or situations give rise to feelings of *loss, powerlessness, depression* and *anger toward oneself.* Also, ask them to consider the feelings and thoughts that arise from relating *acceptance* and *power* to specific losses in life.

Use the **Life Factors and Loss Feelings** *Example Key* to help students understand the task. First, review the list of life factors that could result in feelings of loss, as indicated on the worksheet. The first, divorce of parents, has been used as the example. Discuss each question and ask students for possible responses. As necessary, expand on student responses. Allow students to work on this worksheet alone or in pairs. When students have finished, ask volunteers to share their ideas.

■ Distribute the **Help for Depression** worksheet and allow students time to read it individually. Point out that talking things out (communication) is a coping skill that professionals can help you do. Discuss various people who can serve as resources. Ask students to locate the phone number of a nearby mental health clinic or other counseling resource as homework. Tell students to keep this list on hand. It could be a useful reference someday for themselves or a friend.

Evaluation

Review responses on the **Life Factors and Loss Feelings** worksheet to assess students' ability to describe feelings that arise from challenging life factors.

Students should continue to write in their journals. They can identify their personal styles of coping and analyze their progress in practicing effective ways of coping.

Teacher Background Information
Causes of Depression

Although there is no one cause of depression, depression often has its roots in early childhood. Usually, the first occurrence of a major depression takes place before age 30. Depression tends to develop over a period of days, weeks, months or even years.

It appears that depression is caused by environmental factors, including psychological stressors and traumatic events, or a biological predisposition to depression. Research supports the theory that some types of depression are genetically linked. That is, we can inherit a chemical imbalance that may cause depression.

The following are some environmental factors, including psychological stressors:
◆ family relationships
◆ alcoholism in the home
◆ physical child abuse in the home
◆ emotional abuse in the home (constant criticism, put-downs, demeaning remarks or comments, inappropriate threats)
◆ mental illness in a family member
◆ divorce
◆ a recent series of family moves
◆ absence of a family member
◆ poor communications at home
◆ broken friendships
◆ trouble with teachers
◆ conflicts with parents

Other environmental factors include traumatic events such as the following:
◆ rape
◆ incest
◆ physical injuries or accidents
◆ major physical illness of self or family member
◆ being beaten up by peers or others
◆ death of a loved one

Environmental factors, including both psychological stressors and traumatic events, have in common the element of loss. Losses occur in such situations as:
◆ poor family relationships
◆ having an alcoholic parent
◆ divorce
◆ rape
◆ a major or chronic illness

In all these cases, something is lost. Perhaps we never had it; however, there is still the acknowledgment of loss. If losses continue without relief, we begin to feel powerless and helpless. These feelings lead to hopelessness and the resultant feelings of despair, which can lead to depression.

CONTRIBUTING FACTORS

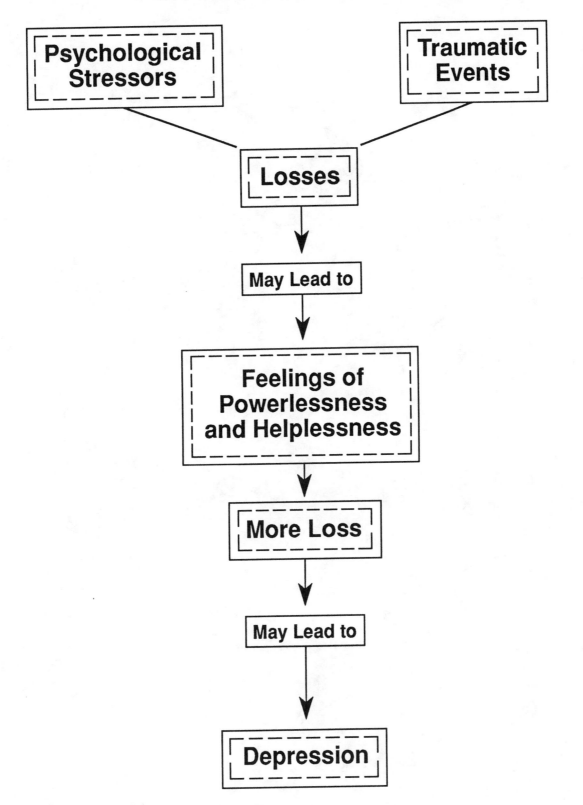

TURNING LOSS AROUND

ACCEPTANCE

Replace the absolute negative side of feelings of loss with acceptance.

"I accept my loss as just that, a life experience of loss— something I can use for growth."

and

POWER

Turn anger and disappointment into powerful resources for growth.

"I can survive pain and loss."

"I am lovable and have much to offer."

"I am not to blame for the actions of others."

Life Factors and Loss Feelings

Directions: Choose a life factor from the list below and describe how it might relate to feelings of *loss, powerlessness, depression* or *anger toward oneself.*

- ❖ divorce of parents
- ❖ death of a loved one
- ❖ family moves away
- ❖ alcoholism in family
- ❖ fight with boyfriend or girlfriend
- ❖ friend moves away
- ❖ money problems
- ❖ problems with grades
- ❖ problems with parents
- ❖ problems with sisters/brothers
- ❖ having a major illness
- ❖ having mental illness in the family

Life Factor: _____

1. What has been lost?

2. When feeling powerless, what might you be thinking?

3. How would you know you were feeling depressed about this event?

4. If you turned your anger on yourself, how might you be thinking, feeling or behaving?

5. What might you be thinking or feeling if you were beginning to accept this loss?

6. What could you say to yourself to turn your anger and disappointment into a powerful resource for growth?

Life Factors and Loss Feelings
Example Key

Directions: Choose a life factor from the list below and describe how it might relate to feelings of *loss, powerlessness, depression* or *anger toward oneself.*

- ❖ divorce of parents
- ❖ death of a loved one
- ❖ family moves away
- ❖ alcoholism in family
- ❖ fight with boyfriend or girlfriend
- ❖ friend moves away
- ❖ money problems
- ❖ problems with grades
- ❖ problems with parents
- ❖ problems with sisters/brothers
- ❖ having a major illness
- ❖ having mental illness in the family

Life Factor: **divorce of parents**

1. What has been lost?
   family unit; family income; family home; one parent physically absent; may lose friends because of self-withdrawal or friends' discomfort

2. When feeling powerless, what might you be thinking?
   There's nothing I can do about it.
   It will never be the same.
   I'm stuck. I'll always feel the way I'm feeling now.

3. How would you know you were feeling depressed about this event?
   feeling worthless; feeling guilty, alone, unhappy; not sleeping; not feeling hungry; thinking about running away; getting drunk or trying drugs

4. If you turned your anger on yourself, how might you be thinking, feeling or behaving?
   It's my fault.
   If only I had...
   They don't love me—no one does—I'm unlovable.
   Drug abuse, reckless driving

5. What might you be thinking or feeling if you were beginning to accept this loss?
   There's nothing I can do about it, because it's my parents' problem.
   I'll find a way to continue knowing and loving them both.
   Things will never be the same, but maybe that's best. Things weren't so great with all those fights.
   As time goes on and I heal, I will feel better about all this.

6. What could you say to yourself to turn your anger and disappointment into a powerful resource for growth?
   I can learn from this experience.
   I've learned to survive pain and loss.
   What others do does not mean there is something wrong with me.
   I am lovable. I am whole and good, and I have much to offer the world.

Help for Depression

The coping skills that you might use for stress management can also help with depression. One skill that becomes particularly important when depression is present is talking. If you are depressed, it is very important to talk to someone about what you're feeling. It's also very important to listen when someone else wants to talk. We all know what it feels like to talk and not be listened to.

It is important to know who your resources are. Who would you talk to if you were troubled and depressed?

Now, what if the first person you choose to talk to is too busy or won't listen? Try someone else. Keep trying until you find someone who will listen. Remember, you are worth it.

Whom to Talk To

It is normal to worry, to be confused, to wonder how to talk to someone and whom to choose and to be concerned about confidentiality. The first step is always the hardest.

A good starting place might be talking to your parents, a teacher, your pastor, rabbi or priest or the school counselor. You could consider seeing a professional therapist (although thinking about talking to a professional therapist, counselor, psychologist or psychiatrist is always difficult). Your friends or someone in your church may also have ideas on whom to talk to.

You can find names and phone numbers in the phone book for a mental health center and therapists or agencies that you can contact. You can call one of these individuals or agencies yourself. You can obtain information about cost, how insurance can pay for the counseling, and whether you need your parents' consent to get counseling. Sometimes a counselor prefers to meet your parents so that the counselor has an idea about your support system at home. If parents are a part of the problem, your parents can get help, too. The most important point is to get the help.

| LESSON 5 | # UNDERSTANDING SUICIDE |

Objectives

Students will be able to identify possible warning signs of suicide.

Students will be able to describe how effective coping skills relate to stress, depression and suicide.

Time

One 50-minute class period.

Overview

Stress and depression exist before a suicide attempt. When we know the relationship of stress and depression to suicide, we can see how coping skills can help prevent suicide. Teenagers need to be aware of some facts about suicide and the warning signs that help determine whether someone is a suicide risk.

In this lesson charts and worksheets are used to illustrate the breakdown of coping skills and the relationship of such a breakdown to stress, depression and suicide. Students work individually on a worksheet that includes some common facts and myths about suicide, then work in small groups to arrive at a consensus about each statement. A class discussion is used to clarify the truth or falsity of each statement.

Teacher Materials and Preparation

MAKE:
✓ Transparency of **Coping Skills Breakdown**.

COPY:
✓ **Coping Skills Breakdown** worksheet for each student.
✓ **Suicide Facts** worksheet for each student.

REVIEW:
✓ **Teacher Background Information**.

Key Points

✓ Stress and depression are important to understand because they are related to suicide.
✓ Stress and depression exist to varying extents before a suicide attempt.
✓ There are many misconceptions about the causes of suicide and about the warning signs suggesting suicide risk.
✓ The warning signs of suicide are unique to individuals. Not everyone who is suicidal will display all of the signs.
✓ Looking for warning signs is only one part of determining suicide risk.

Procedure

■ Remind students of the groundrules established in Lesson 1. Explain that the subject of suicide is difficult. Even the calmest individuals may experience discomfort over this topic, because we are talking about a very real problem that involves death. Tell students that the lessons on stress and depression have been necessary in order to understand suicide. Psychological stressors and depression exist before a suicide attempt.

■ Emphasize to students that effective coping skills are important in preventing the negative effects of stress that can lead to depression and put one at risk for suicide. Display the **Coping Skills Breakdown** transparency, and distribute the worksheet for students to follow along with during discussion. Point out and discuss the characteristics of each stage on the chart. Ask students to interpret the meaning of the chart for themselves, either orally or in writing. *Optional:* Have students create a different illustration of the loss of coping skills (e.g., a tire with a slow leak; plants or flowers slowly wilting).

■ Distribute the **Suicide Facts** worksheet and ask students to complete it. After students have attempted to complete the worksheet individually, divide the class into groups of four or five. Ask students to discuss each statement in their group and come to a consensus on the answer. When all groups have arrived at a consensus, discuss each statement with the whole class and clarify answers as necessary and appropriate. Use **Suicide Facts *Key*** and **Teacher Background Information** as references for this discussion. Conclude by reminding students that it is normal to feel nervous when hearing the warning signs, because they or someone they know may have exhibited one or more of them. Emphasize to students that if they have a concern about someone they know, they should talk to you, the school counselor, school nurse or any other trusted adult as soon as possible.

Evaluation

As appropriate, have students complete the **Suicide Facts** worksheet again and turn it in for teacher review.

Remind students of the coping skills they earlier decided they would practice during this module. Ask them to write a paragraph analyzing their progress in using these skills. Paragraphs can be turned in for teacher review. Students should also note their progress in their journals.

Teacher Background Information
Signs of Suicide Risk

When studying the warning signs of suicide, it is very important to understand that not everyone will display all these signs. Everyone is individual—one sign does not mean a person is suicidal. Looking at warning signs is only one part of determining whether someone is at risk for suicide. We must also consider the person's environment, personal factors, the existence of trauma and change in the person's life and other psychological stressors.

Warning Signs of Suicide Risk

✚ Threats of suicide or statements indicating a desire for death.

✚ A previous suicide attempt after which no counseling was received.

✚ A personality or behavioral change, such as apathy, moodiness, a sudden change from depression to happiness or euphoria.

✚ Depression, including crying, insomnia, hypersomnia, increase or decrease in appetite, irritability, lack of energy.

✚ Giving away of personal belongings.

✚ Excessive use of alcohol or other drugs.

✚ Excessive risk taking, accident proneness or other life-threatening behaviors.

✚ Disruptive or rebellious behaviors, which may be a disguised cry for help.

✚ Truancy or running away from home.

✚ Preoccupation with aspects of death or the impact of death on others.

✚ Poor grades; underachievement.

✚ Overachievement; difficulty in handling failure, disappointment, rejection.

✚ Self-deprecating statements; putting oneself down.

✚ Self-destructive or self-punishing behaviors; self-mutilation.

✚ Neglect of personal appearance.

✚ Leaving notes, diaries, letters where they can be found and read by others. The contents of such writings usually suggest suicidal thoughts or feelings of despair and hopelessness.

✚ Social isolation; lack of close friends; withdrawal from friends or usual social activities; loss of interest in hobbies, sports, job or school.

Reminder: **One sign does not mean someone is suicidal.** Consider the signs, the person's environment, the existence of traumatic events or recent changes in the person's life.

Some Statistics

✛ Suicide is the second leading cause of death for 15- to 19-year-olds.

✛ Suicide is the third leading cause of death for young people between the ages of 15 and 24.

✛ Suicide is the sixth leading cause of death for young people between the ages of 4 and 14.

✛ The suicide rate has tripled for young people ages 15 to 24 since the mid-1950s.

✛ Nearly 31,000 deaths from suicide occurred in 1987.

✛ Males commit suicide more often than females. Females make more attempts than males.

(National Center for Health Statistics)

Coping Skills Breakdown

Effective Coping Skills	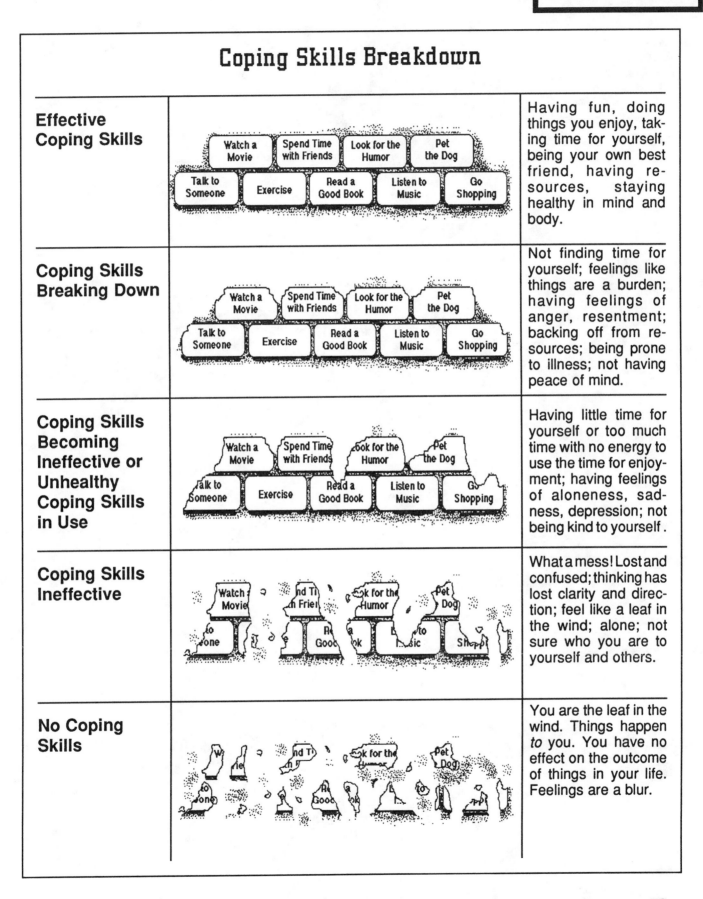	Having fun, doing things you enjoy, taking time for yourself, being your own best friend, having resources, staying healthy in mind and body.
Coping Skills Breaking Down		Not finding time for yourself; feelings like things are a burden; having feelings of anger, resentment; backing off from resources; being prone to illness; not having peace of mind.
Coping Skills Becoming Ineffective or Unhealthy Coping Skills in Use		Having little time for yourself or too much time with no energy to use the time for enjoyment; having feelings of aloneness, sadness, depression; not being kind to yourself.
Coping Skills Ineffective		What a mess! Lost and confused; thinking has lost clarity and direction; feel like a leaf in the wind; alone; not sure who you are to yourself and others.
No Coping Skills		You are the leaf in the wind. Things happen *to* you. You have no effect on the outcome of things in your life. Feelings are a blur.

The diagram panels contain the labels: Watch a Movie, Spend Time with Friends, Look for the Humor, Pet the Dog, Talk to Someone, Exercise, Read a Good Book, Listen to Music, Go Shopping.

Suicide Facts

Directions: Read the statement and put a *T* if you think the statement is true and an *F* if you think it is false.

_____ 1. A suicide attempt is just a bid for attention and ignoring it will discourage another attempt.

_____ 2. There is no such thing as a minor suicide attempt.

_____ 3. The potential for suicide is passed on from one generation to another.

_____ 4. People who attempt suicide are mentally ill.

_____ 5. There is only a very small connection between suicide and alcoholism.

_____ 6. Suicide is preventable.

_____ 7. People who talk about taking their own lives never do it.

_____ 8. Suicide is most common among people who live in lower economic or social classes.

_____ 9. People who attempt suicide want to die.

_____ 10. There is a certain type of person who takes his or her own life.

_____ 11. People who feel suicidal rarely seek medical help.

_____ 12. Suicide is a problem of young people rather than adults.

_____ 13. Once a person has been suicidal, he or she will always entertain thoughts of committing suicide.

_____ 14. Professional people (doctors, lawyers) are not likely to attempt suicide.

_____ 15. Asking a deeply depressed person if he or she has thought about suicide will plant the idea in the person's mind.

_____ 16. Suicide is not the result of a single painful thought, event or remark.

_____ 17. When a depression lifts, the danger of suicide no longer exists.

_____ 18. If a friend confides suicidal feelings or intent, you should always tell someone in authority whom you know will be concerned and will respond.

_____ 19. Suicide occurs without warning.

_____ 20. Nearly all suicide can be prevented.

Suicide Facts
Key

Directions: Read the statement and put a **T** if you think the statement is true and an **F** if you think it is false.

1. **False.** A suicide attempt is not a bid for attention but a most desperate cry for help. It must never be ignored.

2. **True.** There is no such thing as a minor suicide attempt. While the method of attempting suicide may not result in death, the intention behind the attempt must be examined and resolved.

3. **False.** Although suicide does tend to run in families, there is no research to show that it is inherited.

4. **False.** Not all suicides, by far, are mentally ill. Unsatisfied emotional needs that cause feelings of worthlessness and hopelessness can create suicidal thoughts, and the help of a mental health professional should be sought in resolving them.

5. **False.** Alcoholism and alcohol abuse go hand in hand with suicide. Alcohol abuse is a suicide warning sign. Alcoholics are prone to suicide.

6. **True.** Education is one of the best means of prevention. It empowers us to help others and ourselves.

7. **False.** People who talk of taking their own lives frequently attempt to do so. Suicide rarely occurs without warning. Nearly always, there are warning signs of the suicidal state of mind. Talk of taking one's own life is such a signal.

8. **False.** No one economic or social class is more prone to suicide.

9. **False.** A great percentage of people who attempt to take their own lives do not really want to die. In fact, most want desperately to live. However, feeling trapped by the intolerable emotional pain of loss of self-worth and ability to cope, they often feel isolated, desperate, confused and in need of relief. They seek release in death, often not realizing there are other alternatives. Death is a very permanent answer to what is nearly always a solvable, temporary problem.

10. **False.** There is no suicide type. Anyone can become suicidal, because there is no immunity to the feelings that build into suicidal thoughts.

11. **False.** Studies have shown that 75 percent of suicidal individuals visit a physician within the three months prior to their suicide attempt.

12. **False.** Suicide rates rise with age. The peak suicide rate is among older white males.

13. **False**. Although a previous attempt must always be considered if a person continues to show signs of suicide risk, it does not mean that once a person has been suicidal he or she will always be suicidal. Many, many people who have made severe attempts and have received help in defining their problems and resolving their lack of self-worth live happy, productive lives without further thoughts of suicide.

14. **False**. Doctors, lawyers, dentists and pharmacists have high suicide death rates.

15. **False**. To ask a person who seems depressed and indicates life has no worth if he or she has thoughts of suicide *will not* plant the idea in the person's mind. A deeply depressed or distraught person probably already has such thoughts, and asking such a person about suicide intent will often lower the anxiety level and act as a deterrent to suicidal behavior by allowing the person to talk about his or her problems and release pent-up emotions.

16. **True**. Suicide results not from one single cause but from a complexity of causes. Suicide results from a buildup of unresolved negatives that wears away the ability to cope, with the actual suicidal act triggered by a final negative.

17. **False**. Suicide risk is greatest in the three months following recovery from a deep depression. Sometimes a sudden improvement may occur because the person has made the decision to die. The decision may have caused a lift in the person's mood. This is often confused with improvement.

18. **True**. *Never* keep a confidence of someone's suicide intent. Share your concern with a teacher, counselor or parent. It is better to risk the friendship than risk the friend.

19. **False**. Most people plan their suicide and leave clues indicating they are suicidal.

20. **True**. Suicide can nearly always be prevented. Prevention is usually a matter of the right person having the right knowledge at the right time.

Scoring:
18 to 20 ....*Above Average*...You indicate a good awareness of suicide facts.
15 to 17 ....*Good*...Your knowledge is better than most.
14 or less ..*Below Average*...Don't feel bad. Most people know very little about suicide facts.

DETERMINING SUICIDE RISK

Objectives

Students will be able to describe factors that determine suicide risk.

Students will be able to explain why suicide is viewed as a process.

Time

One 50-minute class period.

Overview

Suicide is not an isolated event but a process. The identifiable event that occurs before a suicide attempt is usually only "the last straw." Identifying signs early in the process is a key to suicide prevention.

This lesson emphasizes the importance of verbal suicide warnings by having students read aloud some possible warning statements. A class discussion of suicide risk follows, accompanied by a worksheet listing some of the risk factors. The **Pressure Dome** transparency illustrates the process that can lead to suicide risk.

Students then create their own story or artwork depicting an individual at risk.

Teacher Materials and Preparation

MAKE:
✓ 3 x 5 cards with the **Verbal Warnings of Suicide** on them. Warnings can be pasted or taped, or written or typed on the cards.
✓ Transparency of **Suicide Risk?** worksheet.
✓ Transparency of **Pressure Dome**.

COPY:
✓ **Suicide Risk?** worksheet for each student.
✓ **Contributing Factors to Suicide Risk** worksheet for each student.

Key Points

➤ Suicide is preventable.
➤ Suicide is a process.
➤ Sometimes the process of suicide is accelerated, occurring over days or weeks. Other times it takes longer, involving months or years.
➤ Many people think suicide is caused by a single event. The single event they are referring to is usually only the last straw, the identifiable event that appears just before the suicide attempt.
➤ Many factors can be identified as symptoms, signals or variables before a suicide attempt.

Procedure

■ Explain that you are going to give students a statement to read. Tell them to read the statement with feeling. It can be read with a serious or a humorous tone. (This should be determined by the teacher as appropriate for the situation.) Distribute the 3 x 5 cards with a statement taken from the **Verbal Warnings of Suicide** teacher page. Since there probably are not enough statements for every student in the class, give a card to every other student or distribute them randomly. Give students a few minutes to plan how to express feeling when reading their statements. Students may want to ask for advice from another student who does not have a statement to read. Explain that in some cases, the statement needs some event or item to be filled in. For example, in the statement *If _____ happens, I'll kill myself,* students need to provide an event to fill in the blank.

Have students one at a time read their statements with feeling. Move through the statements quickly, pausing only to comment here and there as appropriate for class composure.

When all statements have been read, ask students what they think the purpose of the activity might be. Explain that verbal statements are important clues for suicide risk and must not be overlooked or taken lightly.

■ Tell students that suicide is to be viewed as a process rather than a singular event. Process can be defined as a series of actions, changes or functions that bring about an end or result. Process involves steps that build to an end.

Suicide risk occurs when many factors are present in the process. Distribute the **Suicide Risk?** worksheet. Use a transparency of the worksheet to guide a discussion about determining the risk of suicide. Have students fill in the sections on their worksheets during the discussion. Use the **Suicide Risk?** *Example* as a resource for the discussion and as a possible key for the worksheet.

As each section of the worksheet (and transparency) is discussed, ask students to provide possible responses. Add to the list in each section as necessary and appropriate. When discussing the possible variables, distribute the **Contributing Factors to Suicide Risk** worksheet to students. Review the variables that enter into a potential suicide risk, including personal and family-related factors and traumatic or major life changes.

Remind students that even good changes in life can be stressful. Any situation in life that requires adjustment can result in stress. Most of the time it also results in some sort of loss. The following are some examples of positive life changes that teenagers may soon experience:
• going away to college
• graduating from high school
• changing jobs (place or work) for higher pay
• finishing an art project

Ask students how each of these life events has an element of loss. Change has an element of loss because we lose the way things were. Change is a fact of life that requires each of us to develop personal coping skills to manage the stress that the change produces. Tell students that it is common to experience depression even when good things happen.

■ Display the **Pressure Dome** transparency. Use it to illustrate how the combination of symptoms, signals and variables can contribute to a suicide risk. Have students label each pressure as a warning symptom (sign), a signal (behavior) or variable (personal/family factors/life change). Write these labels on the transparency. Then ask students what they think "the last straw" means. If they aren't clear about the concept, explain that the last straw is the single event that appears just before a suicide attempt. Some people think that the last straw is the only contributing factor, but in fact suicide is the result of a combination of factors, a process. This concept is important, because when the last straw is seen as the cause, we are led to believe that suicide is magical, that it can jump out and take any of us if something goes wrong.

■ Have students create a story or piece of art that illustrates an individual who could be considered a suicide risk. Students need to show a combination of factors, as discussed. It is important that the individual in the story represent a suicide *risk*—not a suicide attempt. Students may need to complete the story or artwork at home.

Evaluation

Have students explain or illustrate how suicide is a process. This could be written or oral or depicted in a drawing or series of drawings.

Evaluate students' stories or artwork for the inclusion of a combination of factors that could represent suicide risk.

Extension

Have students complete their own version of the **Pressure Dome** for the characters in their stories.

VERBAL WARNINGS OF SUICIDE

1. "I've decided to kill myself."

2. "I've had it; I'm through."

3. "I wish I were dead."

4. "I've lived long enough."

5. "I'm calling it quits—living is useless."

6. "I hate my life. I hate everyone and everything."

7. "The only way out is for me to die."

8. "I just can't go on any longer."

9. "You won't be seeing me around anymore."

10. "If I don't see you again, thanks for everything."

11. "You're going to regret how you've treated me."

12. "It's too much to put up with."

13. "Life has lost its meaning for me."

14. "Nobody needs me anymore."

15. "I'm getting out; I'm tired of life."

16. "If _____ happens, I'll kill myself."

17. "If _____ doesn't happen, I'll kill myself."

18. "Here, take this _____. I won't be needing it anymore."

Suicide Risk?

Symptoms + Signals + Variables = Suicide Risk

Symptoms
(Warning Signs)

+

Signals
(Behaviors)

+

Variables
(Personal and Family Factors, Traumatic Events and Life Changes)

=

Suicide Risk
The existence of a few symptoms, a few signals and one or two variables indicates a potential suicide risk.

Suicide Risk?

Example

Symptoms + Signals + Variables = Suicide Risk

Symptoms

(Warning Signs)

Insomnia, hypersomnia, crying spells, loss of appetite, weight gain or loss, apathy, despondency, moodiness, hostility, anxiety, agitation, indecisiveness or impulsiveness, inability to concentrate, physical or psychological exhaustion, noticeable personality change

+

Signals

(Behaviors)

Threats or hints about self-destruction, preoccupation with aspects of death or impact on others, truancy or running away, disruptive or rebellious behaviors, abuse of alcohol or other drugs, reckless driving, excessive risk taking, accident proneness, sexual promiscuity, social isolation, neglect of personal appearance, putting affairs in order, giving away personal belongings or prized possessions, revising wills or insurance policies

+

Variables

(Personal and Family Factors, Traumatic Events and Life Changes)

See student worksheet **Contributing Factors to Suicide Risk.**

=

Suicide Risk

The existence of a few symptoms, a few signals and one or two variables indicates a potential suicide risk.

Contributing Factors to Suicide Risk

Personal factors include:
- family relationships; the quality of these relationships
- existence or lack of close friends
- alcohol or other drug abuse
- a previous suicide attempt
- impulsive or dangerous behaviors
- school dropout; school underachievement
- perfectionism; difficulty handling failures, disappointments, rejection
- extreme mood swings
- signs of depression; poor appetite, sleep problems, physical complaints.

Family factors include:
- a family history of suicide or a suicide attempt
- a family history of a severe mental disorder
- alcohol or other drug abuse in the family
- poor family communication
- child abuse, incest
- conditions that reduce the family's stability, including financial difficulties
- too much control by family over the teenager's life; no independent decision making allowed
- not enough intervention by the family; parents too permissive, not involved with teenager, teenager makes all or most of his or her decisions; teenager given adult responsibilities

Traumatic events and life changes might include:
- recent loss of a family member through death or divorce
- recent loss of a romantic involvement
- pregnancy
- child abuse, incest, sexual assault
- a family move; new town, new school, new friends; no support system
- earthquake, hurricane or tornado
- any event, situation or change in which loss is involved; in which change and readjustment are involved; in which the dominant theme is loss accompanied by feelings of helplessness, hopelessness and powerlessness

These factors all have one thing in common. They all represent loss of one kind or another. The loss may build and result in feelings of helplessness, hopelessness and powerlessness. These feelings may lead to further depression. As depression sets in more heavily, the person may give up or may become angry at her or himself rather than at others who may be the sources of pain or discomfort. The person is then a risk for suicide. If no intervention (help) takes place, the process toward possible suicide continues.

PRESSURE DOME
THE BUILDUP OF LIFE STRESSES

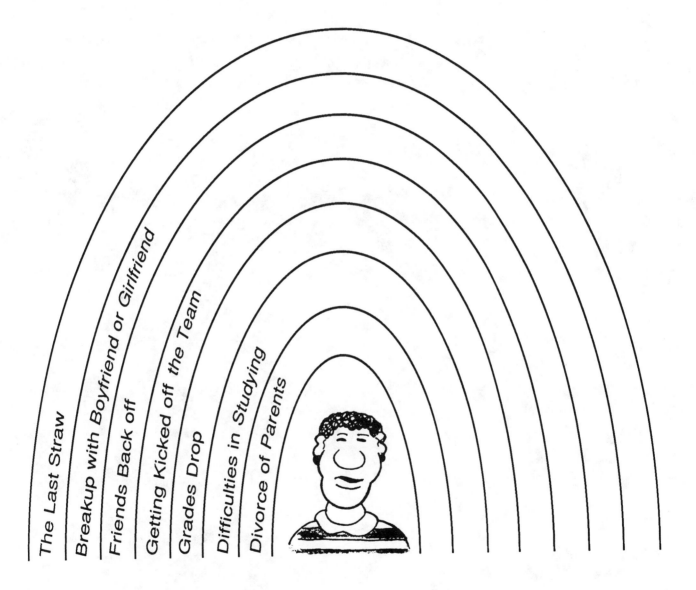

The Last Straw

Breakup with Boyfriend or Girlfriend

Friends Back off

Getting Kicked off the Team

Grades Drop

Difficulties in Studying

Divorce of Parents

LESSON 7

INTERVENTION

Objectives

Students will be able to identify personal and community resources available in crises.

Students will be able to describe appropriate actions to take when they suspect a suicide risk.

Time

One to two 50-minute periods.

Overview

When suicide is viewed as a process, students can see that intervention anywhere during that process reduces suicide risk.

In this last lesson students identify both personal and community resources whom they can consult in times of crisis. A worksheet offers students guidelines to follow in dealing with a person at risk for suicide. The lesson emphasizes the importance of asking for adult help in such situations. A roleplay helps students experience what it might be like to talk to a counselor.

Teacher Materials and Preparation

HAVE:
- ✓ Overhead projector.
- ✓ Several local phone books available for groups to use to look up resources.

MAKE:
- ✓ Transparency of **Intervention Roleplay** *Key*.

COPY:
- ✓ **Personal Resources** worksheet for each student.
- ✓ **Local Help Sheet** for each student.
- ✓ **Basic Tools of Intervention** worksheet for each student.
- ✓ **Intervention Roleplay** for each student.

Key Points

➤ There are basic guidelines for intervention.

➤ Personal resources are people in our lives who can be consulted in times of crisis.

➤ Resources exist in all communities to provide professional help and intervention.

➤ The best time for intervention is before a crisis. The establishment of effective personal coping skills is the best intervention.

➤ Teenagers need to recognize the importance of getting help from a trusted adult if they feel someone may be a suicide risk.

Procedure

■ Write PERSONAL RESOURCES on the board. Ask students to brainstorm possible resources. List them on the board under people to talk to. They might include the following:

parents	minister	therapist
friends	rabbi	athletic coach
teachers	priest	adult friend
school nurse	hotline worker	school counselor
relatives	principal	family physician

Distribute the **Personal Resources** worksheet. Have students review the list and check the boxes indicating the personal resources they have in their lives. They might list other categories of people at the bottom of the page, as appropriate.

Have students list in their journals specific people (at least first names) whom they could talk to in a crisis. It is important for teenagers to identify at least two or three people whom they feel comfortable talking to about difficult things. Encourage students to include at least one trusted adult among the two or three people on the list. Explain that just going through the exercise of listing the resource people available in their lives is an important coping activity. From time to time it is helpful to identify people in our lives who can serve as personal resources during times of crisis.

■ Write COMMUNITY RESOURCES on the board. Explain that one of the functions of a community is to provide help to its members when necessary. Just as communities provide assistance in the form of police protection and fire control, most communities also provide crisis intervention services. These services are often at the county level. The crisis intervention resources available locally are usually listed prominently in the local phone book, often on the first or second page.

Have small groups of students look up phone numbers in local phone books and complete the **Local Help Sheet**. Each group should report to the class the resources its members identified. Students should add entries to their **Local Help Sheets** as new resources are identified by other groups.

■ Write INTERVENTION on the board. Ask students for a definition. As appropriate, explain that it means to intervene or to step in and provide help when needed. In the case of suicide, as with other problems, it is best to intervene or step in with help early in the process. If a suicide risk is suspected, friends, family, teachers, counselors or members of the clergy should not agree to hold information confidential. Since intervention means to step in and prevent a crisis, it usually requires telling someone else about the suspected suicide risk. An important aspect of intervention is knowing where to get help and how to help.

Distribute the **Basic Tools of Intervention** worksheet to students. Present a mini-lecture based on the worksheet, stressing the highlighted points. Have students suggest possible constructive statements they could make that might encourage a friend to get help.

■ Explain that the purpose of the next activity is to show students what an intervention discussion might be like. It is a situation in which a young person in crisis has sought help from a counselor.

Divide students into groups of four or five and give each student a copy of the **Intervention Roleplay**. Tell students that the roleplay is an example of a dialogue between a teenager and a counselor. Two students in each group should read the roleplay while the rest of the students follow along on their worksheets, looking for examples of suicide warning signs and intervention statements. After the roleplay students should work together in their small groups to identify the warning signs (by underlining them) and the intervention tools (by circling them).

Lead a class discussion about the roleplay. Use the transparency of the **Intervention Roleplay *Key*** to point out to students the warning signs and interventions used. Ask students how they felt about the counselor's role. Discuss students' observations about the dialogue and the intervention statements used by the counselor.

Evaluation

Have students write a short paragraph describing what they would do if they thought a friend was a suicide risk. Assess their descriptions for appropriate actions as outlined in **Basic Tools for Intervention**.

Review the students' completed worksheets listing personal and community resources and return them to students. Suggest that students keep these worksheets for future personal reference.

Remind students of the journal activity on coping skills. Have them make a final analysis of their personal progress in identifying and practicing coping skills. Suggest that they continue their journals to help them better understand themselves and to determine the coping skills that work for them. Effective coping is a lifelong skill that can greatly contribute to the quality and happiness of life.

When all students have completed the assignment, ask for volunteers to share their feelings. Provide positive reinforcement for all comments, yet remind students that the best intervention starts with themselves. Establishing positive coping skills can help students deal effectively with the stress in their lives.

Personal Resources

Directions: Read the list below and check those boxes where you have someone you can talk to and can use as a personal resource. Just going through the exercise of identifying personal resources is an important coping skill.

Types of people	*Check the box for each category where you have someone you could talk to*
parents	☐
teachers	☐
principal	☐
school counselor	☐
school psychologist	☐
aunts, uncles, other relatives	☐
adult friend	☐
athletic coach	☐
school nurse	☐
family physician	☐
school secretary	☐
local health clinic	☐
minister, priest, rabbi or other spiritual resource	☐
friends	☐
den leader or scout leader	☐
band instructor	☐
head of local club or organization to which you belong	☐
parents' friends	☐
friends' parents	☐

Local Help Sheet

Directions: When you need help with a problem or when someone you know does, here are some people who can help. Community resources vary from place to place. Complete this list with the right numbers for your community.

Agency	*Phone Number*
Mental Health Center	_____
Local Police	_____
County Department of Social Services	_____
Poison Control	_____
Local Health Department	_____
Local Hospital	_____

Hotlines

☎ Suicide .... _____

☎ Runaway .... _____

☎ Crisis .... _____

☎ Domestic Violence (family violence) .... _____

☎ _____ .... _____

☎ _____ .... _____

☎ _____ .... _____

Other

_____ .... _____

_____ .... _____

_____ .... _____

Basic Tools of Intervention

You are a very important part of intervention with a friend who may be suicidal. First, trust your gut reaction. What are you feeling about your friend? Do you feel his or her helplessness, confusion, depression, isolation? If you do, that's good. That means you're feeling with him or her. Trust those feelings and let your feelings work for you to react. If you feel your friend is at risk and might do something harmful...*react.* Don't allow yourself to be convinced that you are overreacting or that somehow you are mistaken. Overreaction is better than no reaction. The worst thing that could happen is that you are wrong.

When you listen to someone who is experiencing emotional pain, it is normal to feel his or her pain, distress, sadness and despair. This is supposed to happen. It is part of the process of this person's unburdening his or her load. You temporarily act as a container for the person's feelings. Note that your role as a container is only temporary; don't hang on to the other person's feelings.

DO

1. *Listen.* What is the person saying? What is the feeling of what's being said? If suicide is mentioned, discuss the threat openly and calmly. How would the person plan to commit suicide? Is there a detailed plan, or is the threat open-ended? A detailed plan indicates an immediate risk. Most people contemplating suicide are honest about their intent, a plan or lack of a plan.

Let the person know you understand how he or she feels, that the person is heard. We can do this with statements like:

- "You feel..."
- "It sounds like you are feeling...."
- "You seem to be feeling..."

2. *Let the person know that you care and that you want to help.* Suggest alternatives and options. Assure the person that help is available. People seek counseling all the time. It helps to have an objective third party. Explain that you would seek help if you were feeling desperate and helpless. If the person rejects your suggestions, don't pressure him or her.

Statements and actions that show you care include:

- "Help me understand..."
- "I really can see..."
- "I know what you feel..."
- "It must feel awful."
- "That must hurt a lot."
- "You matter to me."
- "What do you think...."
- "It wasn't your fault."
- "Let me know..."
- Have box of tissues handy.
- Use the person's first name.

The following statements can assure the person that help is available:

"I think it might be good to talk to someone."

"I know a counselor who has helped my friend."

3. *Let an adult know of the threat and your concern.* Such an adult may be a family member, teacher, school nurse, school counselor, a member of the clergy or an adult friend. Pick someone who you know will respond in a supportive, caring manner. If the risk feels immediate, the help must be immediate. Get the person to go with you to the counselor's office, nurse's office, etc.

4. *Remove all things that could be used in a suicide.* If you are talking with someone who has a gun or something else that could be used to commit suicide, don't leave him or her alone. Use whatever means you can to get someone else to help.

DO NOT

1. *Try not to act shocked or embarrassed* by what the person is telling you.

2. *Do not say things like "You must be joking" or "You must be crazy."* Such statements are not helpful. A person will feel more alone and alienated if dealt with in this manner.

3. *Do not tell a person how much better off he or she is than others* or that he or she has no reason to consider suicide.

4. *Do not preach or dwell on how bad others will feel.* This could be part of a goal the person secretly wants to accomplish.

5. *Do not tell the person to quit feeling sorry for himself or herself* or to get his or her head together and use willpower.

6. *Don't be critical or make judgments about the problems or feelings.* The pain is real no matter what the problem.

7. *Never leave a person alone who is having intense suicide thoughts.*

8. *Don't try to control the person yourself.*

AGAIN

→ DO GET HELP—TELL AN ADULT OF YOUR CONCERN!

→ DO NOT PROMISE NOT TO TELL ANYONE. If you suspect a suicide risk, you must tell a trusted adult and do everything you can to see that the person gets help.

Intervention Roleplay

Directions: This is an example of a dialogue between a teenager and a counselor. As you read the dialogue, look for examples of suicide warning signs and intervention tools. Underline the warning signs and circle the intervention statements and actions. Discuss your findings with your group.

Jason: I just don't know anymore. I hate life. I hate, hate, hate. Who does Mary think she is anyway? And that new guy Chris, I feel like killing him. It's either him or me. I can't stand feeling this way. I can't sleep at night. I just want off this planet. I don't even know why I was born.

Counselor: It sounds like you're feeling very upset, angry and hurt.

Jason: You bet I'm angry and hurt. I don't know how she could do that to me, and that Chris! You know, I just hate life, I don't want to live anymore. Really, I think death would be a relief right now.

Counselor: I really can tell you are feeling very hurt and confused right now. Help me understand what has happened. What's going on with you and Mary?

Jason: She went out on me. How could she do that to me? I thought everything was fine, and then I heard she was with Chris Friday night. She told me she was going to be studying. I don't want to live anymore. I'm so embarrassed. You know what everyone is going to say at school on Monday. And my mom, she said, "You'll get over her and find someone else." Boy, she has no idea about anything. I don't want someone else. I hate Mary, why did she do that? *(Jason starts to cry.)* I feel like I'm dying. I don't even feel pain anymore. Look. See this. *(Jason shows the counselor where he used a razor blade to cut into his arm in three different places.)* It didn't even hurt. I must be real sick—going nuts or something.

Counselor: I really can see how you are hurting. Anytime we stop feeling physical pain, anytime we want to hurt, like cut ourselves, it means "Hold on, I'm really stuck right now." I know that what you are feeling hurts real bad. Did you and Mary have a fight?

Jason: Yes. She said she wanted to date other guys, that we are too young to be so serious. You know, she's leaving for college next year, and I still haven't figured out what I'm going to do. I understand what she means, but having

her leave me—I'm not sure I can handle that. I feel so alone, I don't have anything without her.

Counselor: I know. It does feel awful to lose someone you really care about.

Jason: It sure does. *(Jason hangs his head and cries.)*

Counselor: Good, Jason, the tears help. They help let out the pain. *(The counselor hands a box of tissues to Jason.)*

Jason: You know what?

Counselor: What, Jason?

Jason: My dad left me when I was five. I can still remember the day. I came home from school and the T.V. was gone, a couple of chairs, some paintings, his gun cabinet. He never said goodbye. They never even told me they were getting a divorce. I guess they thought I was too young to notice or something.

Counselor: Where is your dad now?

Jason: In Wisconsin, last I heard.

Counselor: Do you hear anything from him or see him?

Jason: He writes a couple of times a year. I haven't seen him in two years. He has a new wife and other kids now.

Counselor: That must hurt a lot—not seeing him or hearing from him much. He doesn't know what he's missing, not knowing you.

Jason: You know, I haven't thought about that for a long time. How could he leave, go off and remarry and have other kids? It's like I didn't even exist, like I didn't even matter or something.

Counselor: You do matter, Jason. You matter to me. It sounds like your dad has some problems he's never worked out.

Jason: Well, Mom says he was weird. He drank a lot and was always chasing women when he was married to Mom.

Counselor: It does sound like he has some problems. What do you think?

Jason: I think you're right.

Counselor: I bet you have been real angry at your dad. I can think of lots of reasons for being angry. He left you and your mom, and he has had so little contact over the years.

Jason: Yeah, I'm angry, real angry. Funny how you can be real angry at someone and not know it. I spend most of my time being angry at myself.

Counselor: You know, Jason, what happened with Mary is a lot like what happened with your dad.

Jason: *(Pauses.)* I never thought of it that way. Yeah, you're right. I feel a lot the same about both of them—a couple of jerks.

Counselor: Sometimes when we've been hurt by someone real bad, like you were with your dad, it makes us more likely to be hurt by someone else later, because it's like it's happening all over again. Sometimes we think it's going to keep on happening, and then we can start to give up hope, give up on ourselves.

Jason: I can see that. All I've been thinking is that I want to die. It's really not my fault my dad left or that Mary wanted to break up.

Counselor: You're absolutely right. It wasn't your fault then, and it isn't your fault now.

Jason: I guess I've survived the pain and loss of my dad; maybe that will help me live with Mary's breaking up with me.

Counselor: Losing someone you care about is always painful. Healing is a slow process, but knowing you have gotten through such pain in the past helps provide strength to carry on.

Jason made an appointment to see the counselor a few days later and took the phone number for a local hotline. He told the other kids at school that he and Mary broke up—he wasn't very happy about it, but that's the way it was. He called the hotline a few times when he couldn't sleep. He kept up with his appointments with the counselor. He also started to do more things with friends—friends he had drifted away from when he and Mary were together. Little by little he felt stronger. He tried to keep the attitude: "As time goes on, I can heal and I will feel better. I can learn from this experience."

Intervention Roleplay
Key

Directions: This is an example of a dialogue between a teenager and a counselor. As you read the dialogue, look for examples of suicide warning signs and intervention tools. Underline the warning signs and circle the intervention statements and actions. Discuss your findings with your group.

Jason: I just don't know anymore. I hate life. I hate, hate, hate. Who does Mary think she is anyway? And that new guy Chris, I feel like killing him. It's either him or me. I can't stand feeling this way. I can't sleep at night. I just want off this planet. I don't even know why I was born.

Counselor: It sounds like you're feeling very upset, angry and hurt.

Jason: You bet I'm angry and hurt. I don't know how she could do that to me, and that Chris! You know, I just hate life. I don't want to live anymore. Really, I think death would be a relief right now.

Counselor: I really can tell you are feeling very hurt and confused right now. Help me understand what has happened. What's going on with you and Mary?

Jason: She went out on me. How could she do that to me? I thought everything was fine, and then I heard she was with Chris Friday night. She told me she was going to be studying. I don't want to live anymore. I'm so embarrassed. You know what everyone is going to say at school on Monday. And my mom, she said, "You'll get over her and find someone else." Boy, she has no idea about anything. I don't want someone else. I hate Mary, why did she do that? *(Jason starts to cry.)* I feel like I'm dying. I don't even feel pain anymore. Look. See this. *(Jason shows the counselor where he used a razor blade to cut into his arm in three different places.)* It didn't even hurt. I must be real sick—going nuts or something.

Counselor: I really can see how you are hurting. Anytime we stop feeling physical pain, anytime we want to hurt, like cut ourselves, it means "Hold on, I'm really stuck right now." I know that what you are feeling hurts real bad. Did you and Mary have a fight?

Jason: Yes. She said she wanted to date other guys, that we are too young to be so serious. You know, she's leaving for college next year, and I still haven't figured out what I'm going to do. I understand what she means, but having her leave me—I'm not sure I can handle that. I feel so alone, I don't have anything without her.

Counselor: I know. It does feel awful to lose someone you really care about.

Jason: It sure does. *(Jason hangs his head and cries.)*

Counselor: Good, Jason, the tears help. They help let out the pain. *(The counselor hands a box of tissues to Jason.)*

Jason: You know what?

Counselor: What, Jason?

Jason: My dad left me when I was five. I can still remember the day. I came home from school and the T.V. was gone, a couple of chairs, some paintings, his gun cabinet. He never said goodbye. They never even told me they were getting a divorce. I guess they thought I was too young to notice or something.

Counselor: Where is your dad now?

Jason: In Wisconsin, last I heard.

Counselor: Do you hear anything from him or see him?

Jason: He writes a couple of times a year. I haven't seen him in two years. He has a new wife and other kids now.

Counselor: That must hurt a lot—not seeing him or hearing from him much. He doesn't know what he's missing, not knowing you.

Jason: You know, I haven't thought about that for a long time. How could he leave, go off and remarry and have other kids? It's like I didn't even exist, like I didn't even matter or something.

Counselor: You do matter, Jason. You matter to me. It sounds like your dad has some problems he's never worked out.

Jason: Well, Mom says he was weird. He drank a lot and was always chasing women when he was married to Mom.

Counselor: It does sound like he has some problems. What do you think?

Jason: I think you're right.

Counselor: I bet you have been real angry at your dad. I can think of lots of reasons for being angry. He left you and your mom, and he has had so little contact over the years.

Jason: Yeah, I'm angry, real angry. Funny how you can be real angry at someone and not know it. I spend most of my time being angry at myself.

Counselor: You know, Jason, what happened with Mary is a lot like what happened with your dad.

Jason: *(Pauses.)* I never thought of it that way. Yeah, you're right. I feel a lot the same about both of them—a couple of jerks.

Counselor: Sometimes when we've been hurt by someone real bad, like you were with your dad, it makes us more likely to be hurt by someone else later, because it's like it's happening all over again. Sometimes we think it's going to keep on happening, and then we can start to give up hope, give up on ourselves.

Jason: I can see that. All I've been thinking is that I want to die. It's really not my fault my dad left or that Mary wanted to break up.

Counselor: You're absolutely right. It wasn't your fault then, and it isn't your fault now.

Jason: I guess I've survived the pain and loss of my dad; maybe that will help me live with Mary's breaking up with me.

Counselor: Losing someone you care about is always painful. Healing is a slow process, but knowing you have gotten through such pain in the past helps provide strength to carry on.

Jason made an appointment to see the counselor a few days later and took the phone number for a local hotline. He told the other kids at school that he and Mary broke up— he wasn't very happy about it, but that's the way it was. He called the hotline a few times when he couldn't sleep. He kept up with his appointments with the counselor. He also started to do more things with friends—friends he had drifted away from when he and Mary were together. Little by little he felt stronger. He tried to keep the attitude: "As time goes on, I can heal and I will feel better. I can learn from this experience."

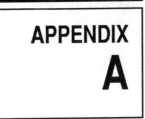

APPENDIX
A

PROGRAM IMPLEMENTATION

Teacher and School Personnel Inservice

A full suicide prevention program involves an inservice training for all teaching, administrative and support staff. It is recommended that such training be facilitated by *both* an educator (teacher, administrator or school nurse) and a trained mental health professional who is familiar with this curriculum and has a solid background in suicide prevention. The following outline serves as a framework for an agenda for the training. Specific content for aspects of the outline can be found in the introduction to the module and within the module's lessons.

Training Outline

I.   Introduction
    A. Purpose of staff inservice training on *Understanding Depression and Suicide*
    B. Suicide statistics
    C. Description of the learning activities within the lessons
    D. School suicide policy

II. Understanding stress as a factor in depression and suicide (refer to Lesson 2)
    A. The meaning of stress
    B. Types of stress
    C. Sources of stress
    D. Healthy and unhealthy coping skills

III. Understanding the role of depression in suicide (refer to Lessons 3 and 4)
   A. The meaning of depression
   B. Symptoms of depression
   C. Loss, powerlessness, depression and anger as related to the process of suicide
   D. Help for depression

IV. Determining suicide risk (refer to Lessons 5 and 6)
   A. Warning signs of suicide risk
   B. Breakdown of coping skills
   C. Factors affecting suicide risk

V. Intervention (refer to Lesson 7)
   A. *Do's* and *Don't's* of intervention
   B. Communicating with a student who is talking about suicide or showing signs of suicide risk
   C. Community resources and referral procedures

VI. Resources (Appendix B)

VII. Bibliography (Appendix C)

Parent Awareness Session

Parents should be notified about learning activities related to suicide. Before beginning any lessons, a parent awareness session should be held. Typically, two hours is enough to present the program and allow time for questions.

A parent session is most successful when conducted by an educator and a mental health professional who is trained in depression and suicide prevention. Parents often present the most difficult therapeutic questions, and a parent session typically is more highly personalized.

Parent Awareness Session Outline
I. Introduction
   A. Brief introduction of presenters
   B. Overview of content
   C. Purpose of parent awareness session
   D. Suicide statistics
II. Understanding stress as a factor in depression and suicide (refer to Lesson 2)
   A. Types of stress
   B. Sources of stress
   C. Healthy and unhealthy coping skills

III. Understanding the role of depression in suicide (see Lessons 3 and 4)
   A. The meaning of depression

B. Symptoms of depression
C. Loss, powerlessness, depression and anger as related to the process of suicide
D. Help for depression

IV. Determining suicide risk (refer to Lessons 5 and 6)
  A. Warning signs of suicide risk
  B. Breakdown of coping skills
  C. Factors affecting suicide risk

V. Intervention (refer to Lesson 7)
  A. *Dos* and *Don'ts* of intervention
  B. Community resources and how to use them
  C. When to get help
  D. What parents can do to help
    1. Know your child—his or her lifestyle, stresses, support systems and coping skills.
    2. Do not ignore suicide threats by your children.
      * Presenter may want to roleplay an interaction between a parent and a child demonstrating that the child is heard and the parent is taking responsibility for seeking further understanding and help.
    3. Get help for your child even if you are unsure of the seriousness of the problem. Know what help is available in your community.
    4. Be involved, be supportive, stay involved in your child's life.

VI. Bibliography (Appendix B)

VII. Resources (Appendix C)

School Suicide Policy

Few schools are prepared to handle the crisis of a suicide by one of their students. It is helpful to give consideration to the formation and implementation of a school suicide policy. If decisions regarding policy are made before a crisis occurs, there will be an increased chance of the crisis being handled more smoothly, with less overall stress for the school, classmates and family. In establishing a school suicide policy, some important considerations need to be kept in mind.

Establish a Crisis Team

A team approach has the advantage of bringing together a variety of professional backgrounds for varied input and ideas. The team's purpose is to establish policy, to provide intervention and support and to keep appropriate channels open between the community, school, parents and students. Additionally, the team can serve as a resource to staff and parents and for follow-up purposes.

Members of the team might be from the community, local mental health center, school (school nurse, counselor, etc.), social services, peer counselors. The function of the team is to meet regarding high-risk students, suicide attempts by students or a suicide by a student or family member.

Establish Policy and Procedures
Policies and procedures must adhere to state laws and recommended guidelines. They might include the following:
- referral procedures
- confidentiality policy
- guidelines for a crisis interview
- development of an intervention plan
- procedures for in-school crises versus after-school-hours crises
- policy regarding how the school will address the death of a student by suicide

Conduct Workshops and Inservice Trainings
It can be very useful to hold workshops for staff on varied mental health and intervention topics. The mental health center in many communities is available to help educators organize training and workshops. Other professionals in the private sector are also available to assist or offer resources for assistance.

Additional Program Strategies
Many additional strategies are available to obtain community, school, parent and student involvement. Below are some sample ideas that are preventive in nature and greatly complement an already existing suicide prevention program. Educators may want to consider some of these additional components.

New Student Programs
The new student is under stress because of relocation of the family and the need to adapt to a new setting. A new student program can help students deal with stress and make adjustment easier.

Program highlights might include the following:
- Assign a counselor or teacher to the family and new student to assist on a personal level with the transition of moving.
- If the school has a peer counseling program, assign a peer counselor to the new student. The peer counselor can assist in many ways, including building orientation, meeting new friends, becoming involved in extracurricular activities and meeting teachers.
- Assign a family or parent to the new student's family to provide community information and to serve as a first friend.

Peer Counseling
A peer counseling program is an excellent preventive strategy. Peer counselors can be trained

to identify high-risk student behavior and to offer peer support and encourage a referral for additional help. Educators may want to consider adopting a peer counseling program.

Divorce Adjustment Groups

Often children involved in the divorce of their parents are experiencing a great deal of stress. A group offers a place for students to share their feelings with others who are also involved in the losses and the stress of a divorce. School counselors may find it helpful to organize and conduct divorce adjustment groups as a preventive strategy.

Stress Awareness Programs

Stress plays an increasingly important role in the physical and psychological well-being of our youth. A program for stress management can be important in suicide prevention. Successful stress management programs often include lessons on the causes of stress, stress management techniques, assertiveness training, relaxation training and time-management concepts. (Educators may want to consider using **Entering Adulthood: Balancing Stress for Success**, another module in the Contemporary Health Series from ETR/Network Publications, which deals with these concepts.)

Decision-Making and Refusal Skills Programs

Decision-making and refusal skills programs have been found to be very important in education to prevent alcohol and other drug abuse. Schools that do not already have such a program may want to consider adopting one.

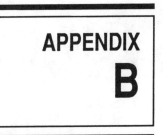

APPENDIX
B

RESOURCES

American Association of Suicidology
2459 S. Ash
Denver, CO 80222
(303) 692-0985

National Center for Health Statistics
3700 East-West Highway, Room 157
Hyattsville, MD 20782
(301) 436-8500

National Institute of Mental Health
Public Inquiries Section, Room 15C05
5600 Fishers Lane
Rockville, MD 20857
(301) 443-4515

Youth Suicide National Center
204 E. Second Avenue, Suite 203
San Mateo, CA 94401
(415) 347-3961

REFERENCES

Alcohol, Drug Abuse and Mental Health Administration. 1989. *Report of the secretary's task force on youth suicide,* DHHS Pub. No. (ADM) 89-1621. Washington, D.C.: Superintendent of Documents, U.S. Government Printing Office.

Alvarez, A. 1973. *The savage god: A study of suicide.* New York: Bantam Books.

American Heritage Dictionary. 1982. Boston: Houghton Mifflin.

American Psychiatric Association. 1980. *Diagnostic and statistical manual of mental disorders* (3rd edition).

Bolton, I. 1983. *My son. My son.* Atlanta: Bolton Press.

Durkheim, E. 1985. *Suicide.* New York: Scholastic Inc.

Gernsbacher, L. M. 1985. *The suicide syndrome.* New York: Human Sciences Press.

Giovacchini, P. 1981. *The urge to die: Why young people kill themselves.* New York: Macmillan.

Haim, A. 1974. *Adolescent suicide.* New York: International University Press.

Hoff, L. A. 1986. *People in crisis.* Menlo Park, Calif.: Addison-Wesley.

Joan, P. 1986. *Preventing teenage suicide.* New York: Human Sciences Press, Inc.

Klagsburn, F. 1976. *Too young to die: Youth and suicide.* Boston: Houghton Mifflin.

Leogrande, E., and G. Alpert. 1975. *Second chance to live: The suicide syndrome.* New York: Da Capo Press.

Mack, J. E., and H. Hickler. 1981. *Vivienne: The life and suicide of a young girl.* New York: The New Library.

Madison, A. 1978. *Suicide and young people.* Boston: Houghton Mifflin.

Menninger, K. 1938. *Man against himself.* New York: Harcourt, Brace and World.

Plath, S. 1971. *The bell jar.* New York: Harper & Row.

Shneidman, E. S. 1967. *Essays in self-destruction.* New York: International Scientific Press.

Smith, K. The youth suicide crisis in perspective. Paper presented at annual meeting of American Association of Suicidology, May 1984.

Sneidman, E., and N. Farberow. 1957. *Clues to suicide.* New York: McGraw-Hill.

Spain, D. 1974. *Post-mortem.* New York: Doubleday.

Sudak, H. S., A. B. Ford, and N. B. Rushforth. 1984. *Suicide in the young.* Boston: John Wright Publishers.

Wekstein, L. 1979. *Handbook of suicidology.* New York: Brunner-Mazel.

Wells, C. F., and J. R. Stuart. 1981. *Self-destructive behavior in children and adolescents.* New York: Van Nostrand Reinhold.

About the Author

Nanette D. Burton, MA, has been a psychotherapist and consultant for the past fifteen years. Her specialty is child, adolescent and family therapy. She has had extensive experience working in numerous school districts and Headstart programs in southern Colorado. Her expertise in education involves work as a mental health consultant, developer of numerous prevention programs and inservice trainings about child development, child psychology, discipline and suicide prevention. She developed a successful K-12 suicide prevention program that has been in use in Colorado since 1986.

Ms. Burton has taught classes in child psychology for the lay population and professionals and is a member of the American Association of Suicidology and founder of the San Luis Valley Association of Mental Health Professionals.

Reviewers of
Entering Adulthood: Understanding Depression and Suicide

David W. Champagne, EdD
Associate Professor
Administration and Policy Studies
University of Pittsburgh
Pittsburgh, PA

Joyce Fetro, PhD
Research Associate
ETR Associates
Santa Cruz, CA

Ric Loya, MS, CHES
Health Teacher
Huntington Park High School
Huntington Park, CA

Gary McEnery, PhD
Psychotherapist/Educational Consultant
Erie, PA

Julie Taylor
Associate Training Director
ETR Associates
Santa Cruz, CA

Dale Zevin, MA
Author/Educational Consultant
Santa Cruz, CA